WOULD YOU LIKE TO GO BIG?

How To Increase Initial Customer Value, Without Sacrificing Life Time Value

by Ryan Chapman

1st Edition 2012

Copyright © 2012 by Market Genius, LLC.

Published by Market Genius, LLC.
145 Vallecitos De Oro, Ste 203, San Marcos, CA 92069

Ryan Chapman
145 Vallecitos De Oro, Suite 203, San Marcos, CA, 92069

Printed in the United States of America

To my always supportive wife, Susan who has always believed in me, even when she had no evidence that she should & the children she brought me.

To my brother Trent who has always kept me pointed in the right direction & saw my potential even when it was a bit rough around the edges.

CONTENTS

Introduction

GO BIG!

I'm sad to say I've heard the phrase, *"Would you like to go big?"* more than once. In it's usual context it has more to do with growing your waste line than your bank account, but it is a context that most are familiar with.

Interestingly enough, to the sales minded individual, after deciding on the title of this book I did some market research (*i.e. I went through the drive through of several fast food chains to listen to their up sell phraseology*) and found that most had raised the bar on the up sell.

Instead of asking if you'd like to upgrade your order, they use a double bind and ask you HOW you want to upgrade your order. *"Would you like to make that combo a medium or a large?"*

Ingenious on the part of the fast food chain, unfortunate for their customer's waste line and health.

However, since this book is not about the merits of fast food, but rather how to increase initial customer value without sacrificing life time value, let's reposition the phrase *"Go Big"* and all it's derivatives.

Going forward the phrase will have a double meaning to you.

"Go Big"

From this time forth, each time you hear, think or say the phrase *"Would You Like To Go Big?"* you will think of one thing and one thing only...Going Big Financially!

In fact, we could upgrade the phrase to include the double bind, *"Would you like to go medium or go LARGE?"*

It's a legitimate question.

What do you want to do? Do you want to go LARGE? Do you want to maximize the value you bring to the market place?

The fact is 99% of all businesses out there are only accepting the lowest of the low hanging fruit. Some struggle to even get that off the tree!

I'll make you a promise, but it will be contingent on your participation.

I promise that you can bump your profit by 50% if you will implement the concepts in this book fully. Some may be able to do far more than that.

There are a couple of caveats. I'm not trying to reduce the power of my promise, so don't take caveats as my way of 'weaseling' or giving myself an escape clause.

Caveat #1: The math in your business has to work.

If you have played a price war instead of differentiating yourself in your market place, well, you'll probably be tempted to do it with your up sells. If you don't charge the appropriate amount, or if you've trained your customers to only judge on price and price alone, it's going to be a tough row to hoe.

Effective marketing and perfect sales choreography are not going to fix bad math on your front end product or service. Up sells COULD fix the math, but it would be contingent on charging the appropriate amount that would produce the profit you've been leaving on the table.

Respect the up sell and it could do well more than 50% increase in your profits, it could bump profits by many multiples.

Caveat #2: Don't cut corners!

This book is designed to be interactive in the sense that I'm going to ask you to write down some answers to key questions that will help you create the real power of up sells in your business.

If you do a half way job of answering the questions, of thinking about the questions, I can't promise too much for you.

I could have gone all crazy and put hundreds of questions in this book to really dig deep, but I understand that less is more. So, I whittled down the questions to a bare minimum without compromising on the evaluation you must go through to really make up sells work for you.

I'm really excited right now.

I'm thinking about the transformation that your business can take as you put up sells to work for you and your customers.

I'm excited about the results you and your business can realize.

I'm excited for your existing and future customers and how much more they'll be able to get from you as the result of your putting up sells to work in your business.

Let's get started!

Chapter 1

HOW TO USE THIS BOOK

I hate long winded business books.

I really detest when an author thinks I need to read through all the research that they've done in order to write the book.

I'd much prefer that the author get the message delivered in 100 pages, if it is possible to do so without compromising the effectiveness of the message, than to take up 300 pages just so the book is thicker on the shelf.

I trust that if an author took the time to write the book, that they probably have the answer, so just give me the answer as quickly and succinctly as you can so that I can solve the problem that prompted me to pull the book off the shelf and begin reading!!!

If you're not of the same philosophy, I'm sorry. You were probably disappointed before you picked this book up anyway!

If you really do want to know more about the research and experience that went into the writing of this book, after you've read every page, give me a call at (760) 452-8555 and we can talk more.

In this book I'm going to give you the meat and potatoes you can put these concepts into action immediately, so let's get started!

I almost skipped this chapter.

I know that seems like a strange confession after I told you '*only meat and potatoes*'.

What I mean is, that I almost popped this chapter into the introduction, but my brother and business partner reminded me that most people don't read introductions. And I really couldn't afford to have you miss this.

In this chapter I'm going to tell you EXACTLY how to use this book.

In chapter 2 we'll begin to identify the core of what your customers really want. If you have ever tried to add up sells to your business, then you might have run up against one of the most common challenges business owner face in the process.

Deciding what to offer as an up sell.

After you read chapter 2 and answer two simple questions at the end of the chapter, you will never have that problem. In fact, you'll know so clearly what to offer when we get to chapter 4, irresistible up sells will practically create themselves.

But don't skip chapter 3, because in chapter 3 I'm going to warn you of the classic mistakes the people make in regards to up sells that KILL lifetime customer value[1].

These mistakes will seem silly after chapter 2, but read chapter 3 anyway. It will just solidify the foundation that you'll use to build your own up sells in chapter 4.

Between you and I, I think that you'll initially be most excited about chapter 4 because you'll be identifying ways that you can increase initial customer value for your own customers, that not only won't hurt life time value, but rather will enhance it dramatically.

DANGER, Mr. Robertson, DANGER!

In earlier drafts of this book I had chapter 4 nearly at the end because I was afraid that if you read the first 4 chapters in the order they now find themselves in this

---

1 Lifetime customer value is the amount of revenue that a customer will generate in your business over the course of time that they are customer of your business. If you don't know what your average lifetime customer value is, hop on it. That is a key metric you must know.

book, you might think you got all you needed and quit reading.

It was only the addition of this chapter as it now stands that alleviated my concerns sufficiently that I was able to move chapter 4 to it's current position.

You see, most business owners get tempted to focus on the short term revenue bump of up sells and stop there. I don't judge harshly because I've been caught in the same trap more than once.

In chapter 5 I'll teach you how to move past just getting a bump in revenue and move to a more sophisticated level of doing business. I'll teach you how to use up sell revenue to move into marketing channels that your competition can't afford.

Marketing channels where the MOST VALUABLE CUSTOMERS live, play and SPEND.

In chapter 6 I'll show you how a business can use a $100 average bump in average initial customer value to nearly DOUBLE their customer base without spending a dime more than their current marketing budget.

At the same time I'll introduce you to the concept of how to determine what you spend to get a customer and how that coupled with lifetime customer value and initial customer value can be used to create a concrete plan to create explosive growth in a company.

All of those concepts are POWERFUL and if you were tempted to stop reading at chapter 6 you and your business would be MUCH better off than you were before you picked up this book. No doubt about that.

However, if you're serious about taking your business to all new heights of profitability, then you really need to study chapters 7-10.

In chapter 7 I'll introduce you to a strategy that few business owners have even considered, much less put to work for them. If you begin using up sells in your business and as a result begin enjoying all the other benefits, but neglect to get what chapters 7-10 offer, I'll be truly saddened.

When you learn how to use up sells to identify your most valuable customers during their initial buying experience, verses waiting months or years to notice how much they are spending with you, you open the doors to a whole new world of opportunities to generate more revenue with fewer customers, while also increasing your ability to strategically generate more referrals.

In chapters 11-13 I share the secrets to success in applying up sells online, offline and in a group sales environment.

Please don't skip chapters or cut your reading short.

I know that some people like to pick through a book; find the chapter they are most interested in and read that first, then go back and read the rest.

Don't do that with this book. Read it at least once all the way through and I promise you'll be glad you did.

Chapter 2

WHAT DO YOUR CUSTOMERS REALLY WANT?

You may be anxious to get to the part where I reveal the secrets of *"Going Big."* You're anxious to boost initial customer value! I'm glad you're excited!

I completely understand!

However, before I can take you there, we have to travel some common ground. It's just the way this life works. So stick with me.

Turn the page carefully, what I'm about to say may shock you...

Your customers and clients do NOT WANT WHAT YOU SELL, OFFER and PROVIDE.

I hope it doesn't feel like a sucker punch or that I'm not aware of YOUR SPECIFIC BUSINESS, because that's the furthest thing from truth.

See, your customer, my customer, they don't want things, even if that's what they insist. They don't want your services, even if they swear on their grandmother's grave that they do!

At a core level, perhaps even subconsciously, what they are really after is a feeling, an emotion.

"What's that Copernicus? They want a FEELING?!?!?"

Yeah, your customer, my customer, they really are after an emotion more than they are after anything else. They just happen to be seeking to get that emotion or feeling by picking up your product or your services.

Now, since I don't know your exact business, I can't tell you exactly what feeling it is they are after. And it could be that your customers are after one or two of a number of feelings, but, at the end of the day, that is what they really want.

Let's take you for example.

You are probably not reading this book because you like the feeling of paper between your fingers, or because you needed another digital book on your e-reader, tablet or smartphone.

I'm confident that you didn't buy this book because you want to know about up sells and the many ways you can use them.

In fact, I'm certain you didn't even buy this book because you want to increase your profits, bank account size and business value (*although I'm sure you'd accept those results*).

No, ultimately there is a feeling that is deeper that motivates your actions and the actions of others. Generally they fall into two categories: avoid pain and attract pleasure.

On it's surface it may seem that this has nothing to do with up sells, but it has EVERYTHING to do with effective up sells.

It's the basis for:

★ WHAT to up sell
★ HOW to price your up sell
★ WHEN to offer an up sell
★ WHOM you ought to offer an up sell to

We all have problems.

Some of our problems cause us real pain.

Pain so intense we'd do anything to get rid of the pain.

We'd start running every morning in the bitter cold. We'd start getting out of bed an hour earlier.

Heck, we'd even read a book about up sells to get rid of some pain.

We all have dreams.

There are things we want so deeply that we'd do almost anything to get it. And if we dug real deep into why we want those dreams we'd find out at the end of the trail, that the ultimate reason we want our dreams is because of the way it will make us feel when we realize them.

If what you bring to the market place has value, then somehow what your bring helps people move closer to their dreams (a feeling of pleasure) or away from their problems (a feeling of pain).

When you're clear on what it is your customers want you'll find increasing initial customer value, without reducing life time value to be EASY, REWARDING and PROFITABLE!

So, let's help you set the stage for a EASY, REWARDING and PROFITABLE life! Let's hit the first two questions!

What problem do you solve for your customers?

Write your answers in the lines following the questions

_____

_____

_____

_____

_____

_____

_____

_____

_____

_____

The problem I solve for readers of this book is: I help them remove the pain of knowing that they could be making more money than they are right now or to go deeper, the pain of not living up to their full potential.

Notice that the problem is referencing a pain and does not include the solution or the "HOW" it's done. That comes later, and needs to be eliminated from the description of the problem your customer has.

When we try and include the solution, our solution, in the description of the problem we warp our understanding of the problem to match the solutions we have in our business right now. The result is we miss the mark and our up sells don't reach their full potential.

Returning to the problem my customers have, and I'm guessing here, but it's a guess based on experience with my clients... There is a deep need to feel like you are realizing your full potential. You won't be fully satisfied with life until you feel like you are operating at your very best.

It's what drives you and keeps you working hard while others goof off.

Sometimes, not always, but sometimes the answer to the next question is really the other side of the problem coin.

What dream do you help your customers get closer to realizing?

_____

_____

_____

_____

_____

_____

_____

_____

_____

In my case, the dream is the opposite of the problem, but that's not always the case.

For readers of this book, the pleasure is feeling like you squeezed every drop of your potential out of life as manifested by an extremely profitable and successful business, while helping customers reach their own goals and dreams.

You may even want that pleasure because it brings with it the accolades of others...their admiration and respect.

Maybe your motivations are less noble and you want to stick it to the person who judged you harshly as *"never amounting to anything"* because you didn't follow their advice or prescribed path to success and happiness.

Of course, I'm just guessing, I could be way off.

Regardless, I'd like you to make sure you take your best guess right now at what attracts people to your product or service at the deepest level you can get to.

Really, this isn't just helpful for creating irresistible up sells. It's the basis for the best marketing and sales pitches. It's the **nucleus** of the conversation you want to get to in all your interactions with your customers.

This is a terrible indulgence, but since I'm writing the book, I'll take it. I can't use or say the word nucleus without thinking of this video clip: http://j.mp/nachonucleus

<-- Scan this QR Code to view the video

...if you have not answered the two questions in this chapter, then you don't have permission to read the rest of the book, *UNLESS*, you just don't have a business yet, then it's OK to keep reading until you get a business, then at that point, you have to come back to this chapter.

Serious.

I mean it.

Answer the questions!

(If you're reading this on an electric do-hickie, then I recommend you don't write your answers in the book. Grab a notebook that you won't loose and keep your answers in the book, written out by hand. Just trust me...)

Chapter 3

4 MOST COMMON UP SELL MISTAKES

More often than not, when I broach the subject of up sells with business owners who have not accepted the virtue of the up sell, I hear only NEGATIVE experiences. Experiences that are used as an excuse for not implementing up sells in their businesses.

To be honest, at first, this puzzled me.

Why is something that's a powerful tool to make your business much more effective, strategic and helpful to customers, tainted with a stigma so dark and ugly???

As the stories come out, without fail, there is a combination of 4 common up sell mistakes that are taking place.

If you commit any of these four up sell sins then I can guarantee there is an underlying theme that you'll need to address before you go any further.

Quit focusing exclusively on the extraction of MONEY from the customer.

If your business is solely focused on increasing initial customer value, or in other words pulling as much money out of your customers as quickly as you can, then you will lose in the long run.

You'll reduce lifetime customer value.

If you don't reduce lifetime customer value because you extract it all out of the customer in the initial transaction without regard to their desire to remove a problem or pursue a dream, then you'll pay with a bad reputation.

Either way you'll lose.

You can quickly detect if your focus is on the wrong thing because you'll make one or more of the 4 common mistakes. But, if you'll answer the questions in Chapter 2 and get real clear on what dream your customers want to realize and or which problem they are trying to solve, it will be very easy to avoid these mistakes and still get ALL the benefits of properly increasing initial customer value.

Classic mistake #1...

Disconnect From Pain the customer wants to get rid of or the pleasure the customer wants to feel.

Have you ever been presented with an up sell and wondered, *"Why are they offering this to me?"*

If that question comes up in your mind, it's most likely because there is a disconnect from the core problem or dream and the offer presented.

To the customer it can feel like they've been had.

Their trust has been violated and whatever relationship they imagined they had formed with your company has been reduced to the perception that they are now a means of creating revenue for your company rather than being a customer who is respected and valued.

PERCEIVED disconnect is a HUGE mistake, and I hope you never, ever make it.

Mistake #2 unfortunately can cause the customer to accidentally mistake a connected up sell as a disconnected up sell, because mistake #2 is...

No Attempt To Connect The Dots

Let's suppose that you went through the exercises in Chapter 2, then skipped to Chapter 4 and created some great and congruent offers that really will help the customer to get what they really want faster and easier.

And so you present the up sells to the customer but you fail to connect the dots on how the offers you've made will help them get closer to what they really want...

What do you think will be the result?

You will run the risk of the customer not connecting the dots and PERCEIVING the offer to be disconnected from what they really want.

Unfortunately, it's NOT the job of the customer to connect the dots. It is YOUR fault if they don't recognize how the offer brings them what they want and as a result feel like they've been taken advantage of by you and your company.

Provide enough copy with logical connecting of the dots, with emotional reasons to back up the decision to say YES to the offer and you can avoid this mistake all together.

Really this mistake is a function of laziness more than improper focus. But since the perception of the customer is the same as if your focus was on the wrong thing (money only), then it made the list of things you must watch out for.

Which leads us to...

Too Many Up Sells

"*Too many*" is a very interesting concept because it's very subjective.

I'm often asked, *"What's the ideal number of up sells to offer?"*

If you want to know all my thoughts on this question and questions like it, read chapter 14.

This question is one of those, *'boil it all down to a thimble full of information for me'* questions. The thimble answer is: there isn't an ideal number for all customers and all situations.

The real answer is:

- ★ How well do your offers match up to the core problem or dream your customer has?
- ★ How well have you connected the dots?
- ★ How well do you detect if a customer is a MVC? (*see chapters 7-10*)

If you can't answer any of these questions well, then you should offer **ZERO** up sells and that may be *too many*.

If you are able to do well at 1 and 2, then 1-3 up sells will probably be safe.

If you can detect and provide up sells based on the customers MVC rating, then you can offer 1-20 up sells safely.

See, if I present to you 1 up sell offer that is congruent, but not a match for you at this time, you'll be complete happy that I thought of you.

If I do it a second time, you're probably still ok, but now you've had to say, *"No."* two times. After having said, *"Yes!"*

once and *"No"* two times you may begin to have mixed emotions.

If I make you say *"No"* again, I may create a negative emotion in you at a time I'd like you to be feeling really good about your decision.

Tony wouldn't be annoyed enough to offer to pay extra to not have up sells offered to him if he only had to say, *"No"* twice.

Instead of a *"Yes"* set, I've created a *"No"* set.

Chapters 7-10 will help you avoid this by paying attention to one of the primary benefits of up sells beyond the bump in initial customer value. And it will help you create up sell offers that can be chained in such a way that will prevent *"No"* sets from becoming long enough that they create a negative emotion in your customer.

I want to point out to you now, since we're discussing emotions, that in Chapter 2 we clearly came to the conclusion that your customer wants an emotion at the end of it all.

If they are after an emotion, then with our sales process we want to strengthen their hope that they will get what they really want by doing business with us.

If you won't put in the effort or get help to identify the ideal up sells and then take the time to structure their delivery in such a way that it will promote and propel the customer toward greater hope, then you will be better off leaving this entire subject alone.

But the great news is, it's easily avoided. Take a little time and effort to think about your customer and what they really want, and how you can help them get it.

Make sure that as you organize up sells, you create long "*yes*" sets and short "*no*" sets. If the order of your up sells follow the concepts in chapters 7-10, you'll be in good shape.

I would be remiss if I didn't point out that a Most Valuable Customer who can and will say yes could be very grateful if you were to offer 10 or 20 up sell offers that moves them toward their desired outcome faster and easier.

Once you've eliminated the mistake of too many offers, don't make the related mistake of NOT offering enough up sells to those who NEED them to feel hope and excitement about their future!

Finally, mistake #4...

Up Sells That Make The Initial Order Seem Incomplete

When you make an offer and your customer buys it, and that is their initial transaction, if your up sell makes the initial order seem obsolete or incomplete, the customer will feel like they were tricked!

That would be the equivalent of tricking someone into going on a date with you. Not the ideal way to begin a relationship.

I suppose this happens all the time with online dating sites where people put up fake photos of themselves only to spring the truth on their would be courter when they finally meet in person.

That relationship isn't going far.

Do me a quick favor and place your finger in the book and close it. Read the subtitle of this book. Do you think we will be protecting lifetime value if we trick people in our attempt to increase initial customer value?

"Hold up Ryan. I wasn't trying to trick them I just wanted to really compel them to take my up sell."

Intention is not the king of the court. Customer perception rules this land, and regardless of what you may be trying to accomplish, make this mistake and you pay big time!

Don't do it. It's simple to avoid!

If you want to keep a good reputation...

If you want to maintain and build trust with your customers...

Don't commit these 4 common mistakes.

Don't present up sell offers that are inconsistent with the problem they want to get rid of or the dream they want to pursue.

Don't fail to connect the dots. Make sure that you clearly explain why each up sell is being presented to them and the benefit they will get out of taking you up on the offer.

Present additional up sell offers only to those who are expressing interest in accelerating or facilitating their journey to alleviating a problem or pursuing a dream.

And finally, make sure that your initial offering is complete without the up sells that follow it.

Up sells should only speed up or make it easier for the customer to get what they want. It should make sense to the customer that they would need to invest more to get what you are offering as an up sell.

If you avoid these mistakes I promise you that not only will up sells give you that bump in revenue you want in your business, but that you will have happier customers who will be grateful you gave them opportunities to solve their problem or reach their dream faster and easier than they would have otherwise!

Chapter 4

CREATING IRRESISTIBLE UP SELLS

I keep a relatively tight ship. Partially because I'm not a great manager of people yet, and then because I'm not entirely fond of large numbers of people and the inherent wasting of time large groups breed.

One of my few employees suggested that there could be a secret set of ratios that could pin point the BEST prices to attach to up sells.

While I'm quite fond of logic and reason, I'm also extremely pragmatic. If there were such a series of ratios, I'm concerned that love of ease would trump love of thought and poor choices would be made in selecting the right price for an up sell and openness to testing would be tossed out the window.

In one of my early successful businesses we began pricing of our product at $297, but quite certain we were below what the market perceived to be the value of our product, we raised the price to $497.

Seeing NO difference in sales, we raised the price again to $797.

Still no difference, so we raised it again to $997.

Still nothing.

$1,297.

Nothing.

$1,497, dramatic drop off.

We ended up pricing the product at $1,497 with 3 equal payments, and a discount to $1,297 if paid in one payment.

We brought thousands of customers in at that price. We made a BIG difference in the industry with what we sold.

If we had settled at $297 or $497 we would have put ourselves out of business quite quickly. Tens if not hundreds of thousands of families would have suffered as a result of our failure to get what we had out into the marketplace.

$1,297 ended up being the perfect price to allow us to learn the business without driving it into the ground.

Before we talk about any special strategies or tricks to pricing, I want you to be firm in your understanding that TESTING TRUMPS ALL.

Further, there is no separating price from what is offered.

You may be able to offer just anything and have a percentage of the people take you up on it, but it will cost you more than you would 'steal' from the unsuspecting.

So, you will NEVER start with pricing.

I understand that I'm cutting contrary to what MOST people want to hear. But I ain't here to whisper sweet nothings to you. I'm hear to tell you the truth. If you start with price or some formula for pricing you won't do as well as you could.

End of sentence.

Start with the problem.

What problem is your prospect seeking to resolve?

What solution are they after?

Your core product or service should be addressing this core need. If it isn't, it may be time for some honest evaluation. It may be time to make some adjustments in you offerings.

The price of your core product should be set by TESTING. Start where the math makes sense and your ability your ability to sell intersect. Then start adjusting until you discover the optima.

Your up sell offers are determined by identifying how far your core product or service gets the customer to the solution they are after.

What else could you do for, or sell your customers that would make it easier or faster for your customer to get the complete solution they are after?

Make your list, because this is the beginning of determining how many and in what order your up sells ought to be structured.

_____

_____

_____

_____

_____

_____

_____

Now write down next to each solution how much you would gladly accept for the up sell offers you've identified based on what we have discussed in this chapter.

First, we want 'speed' solutions.
Then we want 'ease' solutions.

Why? Generally speed costs more than ease, and both have their draw to the MVCs that will be exposed to your offers.

We want the highest priced offers placed first. There are a number of reasons for this, the least of which is way the mind deals with numbers.

There is a psychological concept known as anchoring, which is particularly powerful in relation to numbers and how the mind determines value, especially without well known reference points.

Numerous studies have shown that when a large number is *processed* by a person, a smaller number is perceived to be significantly smaller than had the smaller number been presented without the larger number first.

The important phrase here is PROCESSED. By having our more costly offer shown first, and causing the customer to process the number as they evaluate if the offer is worth the amount presented anchors that number into the mind of the customer.

Now when subsequent lower prices are presented, such as a down sell or lower priced up sell, they look more attractive or price as a criteria becomes a mute issue.

The important point to remember here is that your prices are not set in stone. You can and ought to tweak and test within the range you're willing to accept for what you're offering.

The next common question is:

How many up sells are OK to offer?

The answer is, "*It depends.*"

I introduced this question in chapter 3, but let's dive deeper.

My experience and the experience of marketers I trust and respect have shown that you should avoid any scenario where the customer is required to say, "*No.*" more than 3 times.

This is not a matter of how many a customer will take, but more a matter of how many offers can you place before a customer that will strengthen the relationship with the customer.

If you haven't already picked up on the fundamental approach to sales and business I've espoused, let me state it expressly: The point of a sale is to gain a customer. To contrast this, let me state what it is not. The point of a sale is not to make the sale.

A profound experience can occur when you examine the way you run your business. Are you focused on the sale? Are you focused on the immediate?

I'm the first to admit, you got to make money. There's no point being in business if you aren't making money. But making a single sale can't be the long and short of your business or you won't make it for long and if you do, you'll be working MUCH harder than you need to for MUCH less than you ought to.

What do you do to insure that you will have a long relationship with your customers?

It may not seem like it has anything to do with up sells, if you thought up sells were just about EXTRACTING money from customers.

Up sells will create more revenue. That's a fact. BUT the point of up sells ought not to be *just* creating more revenue up front.

It has to be about creating a stronger bond with your customers by allowing them to purchase and move toward their solution as quickly and easily as **THEY** want to move toward the result they are after.

The other point to remember is that up sells don't have to give ALL the options or offers you can make to your customers in one fell swoop. The strategic benefit to your overall business is what ought to dictate which offers you present.

You want to present no more and no fewer up sells than are necessary to achieve your strategic objective.

Chapter 5

PROFITABLY OUTSPENDING THE COMPETITION

If everyone in your market is paying roughly the same amount to acquire a customer, then what would happen if you could do it for 66% of the cost your competition has to pay?

Let's suppose that it costs you $6 to pick up a new customer, but your competition has to spend $9.

What if you were all fishing in the same pond? In other words, what if you all used the same marketing channels? What would your business look like in a year? In 2 years? What would your competitions' businesses look like?

What if you could take a bigger loss up front than your competition, but you could still make more money per client than your competition?

What if you could afford to spend $12 to get a new customer but your competition could only afford $9. Could that cause your competition to stress? Could it cause them to make some stupid mistakes? Could it leave them up late at night racking their brain to understand HOW you are able to spend so much for a customer???

This is what I call stacking the deck.

And when you stack the deck you always win.

When you employ properly designed up sells into your business and as a result increase the average initial customer value, you effectively stack the deck in your favor.

Not all marketing channels are created equal.

In a recent training I gave on marketing I had all the attendees siting in round tables that seated 6 people to a table.

I had 3 slips of paper that each contained a double headed arrow with a single word handed out to each table. At one end of the arrow there was a plus sign and the other contained a minus sign.

Plus indicated 'more' and minus indicated 'less'.

I asked each table to arrange the arrows so that all would reflect a correct statement at the same time.

The three words were:

★ Competition
★ Ease
★ Value

Our discussion was around the idea that a marketing channel has all three components to it. There was a level of competition that could be expected in the media. That level of competition had a relationship that was either directly or inversely proportional to the ease of participating in that media and the value of the customers that could be obtained from that media.

There was intense debate at each table as they worked to get on the same page. I've included a page designed for you to rip out and cut or rip out the 3 double headed arrows.

Go ahead and do that now. Layout your arrows to represent the relationship between the three concepts.

Of course I'll give you my answer in just a bit, but if you do peek, take a minute to evaluate my answer and see if you agree.

If you have experience marketing in multiple medias, you should be able to draw from your experience (*assuming you were able to successfully get a customer from your marketing and have tracked the revenue customers generated from each media. I have.*)

This page is meant to be ripped out and ripped up, then arranged so that the relationship of the 3 arrows is correctly represented. The answer in a few pages from here!

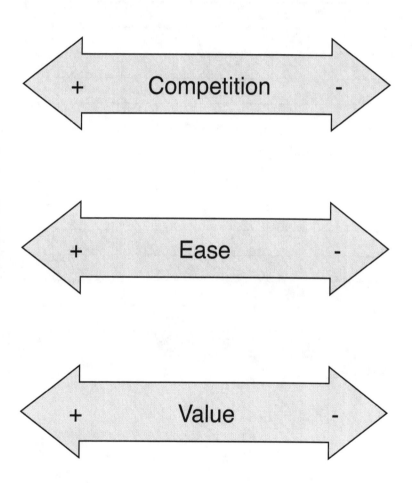

rip along this dotted line

intentionally left blank

Once the attendees arranged their arrows and came to a unanimous decision (*which, by the way, they all did without my giving them the answer I had*), I had an envelope containing ten media channels distributed to each table.

Now, I know that this is by no means an extensive list. It's not even a list of the top 10 by any stretch of the imagination. It happen to be a list of the 10 most common media channels that the particular niche of business owners I was teaching use.

The list was:

- ★ Online: Blogging
- ★ Mailbox: Letters
- ★ Online: Twitter
- ★ Personal Referral
- ★ Online: Facebook
- ★ Online: Craigslist
- ★ Mailbox: Postcards
- ★ Mailbox: Packages
- ★ Mailbox: Greeting Cards
- ★ Professional Referral

I asked them to arrange, as a group, these ten media channels along the arrows they had already laid out. I instructed them to put them in order of easiest to implement to hardest along the 'Ease' arrow first, and then evaluate their position relative to the other two arrows.

They could make adjustments as they debated the merits of each channel relative to the amount of competition and the quality or value of the customer that would come from each media.

I have to say that as a trainer, this type of learning is not only the most powerful for those who participate, but is every instructive to direct and watch.

All in attendance GOT the topic and walked out with a SOLID understanding of which media channels were most valuable and as a result worth their attention.

There were firm commitments to do more in channels that had been neglected because of difficulty.

Due to the nature of the niche and the experience of the group, I did not touch on the impact of up sells to this entire topic, but because that is why we're together right now, I will for your benefit and profit.

The following page is another ripper outer. Tear it out and separate all the media channels into 10 strips of paper. Lay them out on the 3 arrows as instructed above. For the best experience, grab someone who can understand the discussion (like a 12 year old or an entrepreneur with marketing interests) and debate with them why each one should be placed where it is.

Your Ten Media Channels

Online - Blogging

Mailbox - Letters

Online - Twitter

Personal Referral

Online - Facebook

Online - Craigslist

Mailbox - Postcards

Mailbox - Packages

Mailbox - Greeting Cards

Professional Referral

intentionally left blank

My answer for exercise number 1

Competition is directly proportional to value and inversely proportional to ease. In layman's terms; the easier a media is to use, the more competition there is and the lower the value of the customer that comes out of it...generally.

The opposite is also true. The more difficult a media is to use, the less competition there is and the higher the value of the customer that comes out of it...generally.

Unfortunately I have to say *'generally'* because the same folks who have to be told not to eat the silica packets in the box with their new shoes or their dried fruit are also the folks who read a sentence, don't take the time to really understand what all the *'details'* are behind it and then scream like a banshee when they don't get the expected results.

I'm not really too concerned about you, but I'm not quite sure who might accidentally pick up this book when they see it on your desk, in your car or next to your bed.

It's like leaving a loaded gun, extremely powerful in trained hands, but extremely dangerous in the wrong hands...I have to be careful for their sake.

My answer for exercise number 2

I'm not going to tell you what order the ten media channels should appear in for you. Honestly, there will be some variance from niche to niche in the exact order.

Generally my experience has been that the order would have referrals at the top of the value list. Next would come mailbox with the larger and more interesting the piece the higher the effectiveness assuming the copy was up to par. And finally would be online.

Please don't misinterpret me to think that online is pointless as we were able to generate millions in revenue with an online combined with off-line marketing strategy.

The point of this entire discussion.

When you're able to earn more per customer on the front end as a result of strategic placement of up sells and future interaction on the backend due to what the up sells tell you, you can afford to be in media channels your competition simply can't.

When you stack the deck in this manner you put your business in a position to entirely dominate your marketplace because you'll be extracting all the potential from your business that's available to it.

This is called designing your business for ultimate profit and success.

SIDE NOTE on DESIGN

I've been using the word DESIGN occasionally in this book.

Often design is mistakenly considered to be synonymous with STYLE.

STYLE is a temporary fad, which is always changing.

DESIGN, in contrast, is something that solves a problem.

It's timeless.

Obviously, not all designs are equal.

Some designs are quickly thrown together and lack the substance of thought and research that would give them the full title of DESIGN.

I'd like to encourage you to DESIGN your business. Design your up sells. Design your sales process. Design the way you collect revenue. Design the way you grow your business.

Don't allow the next popular approach, gimmick, technique or piece of technology to STYLE your business.

Avocado green was always a bad idea for carpet, regardless of what you thought in the 70's.

Chapter 6

THE KEY TO EXPLOSIVE GROWTH

> *WARNING: When I read this chapter to my most trusted advisor, she told me that it contained too many numbers and calculations and her eyes glazed over.*
>
> *I rewrote the chapter to make it easier to digest, but before you read this chapter eat your Wheaties. If you are not in the mood for concentration, then skip this chapter until you are.*

Present any business that is not already effectively utilizing up sells and I'll gladly sign a contract for 20-25% of the unrealized profits in exchange for structuring, designing and implementing an up sell strategy.

If you want to take me up on that offer, give me a call at (760) 452-8555 right now, and we'll talk.

Seriously. Call me.

"Even if it required a year to do?"

"Absolutely. I call that easy money. You will too!"

Why?

Most companies leave a full HALF of their potential profits on the table.

Your customers WANT to
spend more money with YOU.

They want you to facilitate them getting MORE of what they DESIRE. And they will HAPPILY part with their money when given the RIGHT opportunity at the RIGHT time.

20-25%

I've heard roughly the same figure coming out of *'kitchens'* across the world that are actively using up sells.

20-25% of customers will take you up on a properly constructed up sell. Even more will if you can nail the motivation I asked you to discover in chapter 1.

But before we go any further, I've got to make sure you're solid on WHY you MUST be offering up sells. It needs to be so crystal clear that you won't flake out on us.

No, I'm not calling you a flake. But it happens all too often, so let's just combat the possibility.

Like I said in the warning at the beginning of the chapter, we're going to have to do a little math in order to make it clear why up sells are no longer optional, but REQUIRED for your business going forward.

The easiest reason, and most common reason anyone gets interested in up sells is they want to make more money.

Of course there are the deeper reasons we mentioned in chapter 1, but we'll keep this conversation superficial.

So what kind of money are we talking about with up sells?

Let's look as some real numbers to put this into perspective.

Let's say your average LVoC[2] is $2,400.

And let's say your average CoAC[3] is $200.

I hope that seeing these two real numbers raised the need for another set of data in order to effectively analyze what a difference from up sells can do. You need to know the duration of time that a LVoC is accumulated over, and how it is accumulated.

If the LVoC is a straight line over a 2 year period that would mean that the each month the business picks up $100. That means that if our CoAC is $200 it would take 2 months to break even on the cost of getting each customer.

---

2 Lifetime Value of a Customer
3 Cost of Acquiring a Customer

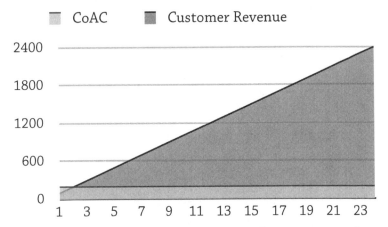

This is important to know about your business. How long does it take to get to break even on your average customer?

Write it down right here:_____

The reason this is such a big deal is it tells you how quickly you can grow your business with the capital you have on hand to work with.

Let me take a step back.

I know that this book isn't going to be able to teach everything there is to know about marketing and business, but some topics are just so tightly intertwined that I can't help it.

Most companies would like to grow.

The reason they want to grow isn't so they can talk about how many customers they have, but so that they can create more profits.

Growth, however isn't as simple as pushing more customers in the front door.

There are three primary areas all businesses have to pay attention to:

1. Bringing new customers into the business.

2. Keeping customers as customers for as long as possible.

3. Reactivating customers who have not done business in a period of time that is deemed as too long.

Returning to the numbers introduced earlier, if we want a business that generates 5 million dollars a year, we know EXACTLY what must be done.

$5,000,000 / ($2,400/2 years) = 4,167 Customers

There is no mystery to what the company must focus on to get what it wants. Bring in, keep and reactivate until we get 4,167 customers.

That is if everything stays exactly the same. If our LVoC stays the same and our CoAC does too.

Considering these two assumptions, that lifetime value of a customer stays the same and that our cost to acquire a customer does too; if we were to adjust either of those two in the process of adding up sells, we could lower the number of customers needed even further.

Go ahead and modify the life time value up a bit. Figure in a reduced cost in customer acquisition by increasing initial customer value by $10 more. How do these small adjustments effect how many customers are needed? You'll see that creating a plan for growth becomes very easy to do when you can incorporate appropriate up sells into the mix.

But for the sake of our discussion will keep these two variables fixed.

Predicting Growth and It's Cost

We can predict and calculate exactly how much capital it will take in order to reach our goal of $5Million...if nothing changes.

The amount of marketing capital in play and the length of time that capital must be tied up can be clearly calculated by multiplying the CoAC by the amount of time it will take to break even.

So if we want to bring in one new customer we need to be prepared to have $200 laid out for 2 months or $400. It's $400 because we don't intend to stop the first month so in order to bring in one new customer each month we'll have to have $400 invested at any point in time.

Yeah, you'll get back $100, in this scenario, the first month, but realistically we need to delay that a month to represent the time it takes for the books to settle and to accommodate for time from marketing sent, prospect raises hand, initial purchase made.

I hope that you are already translating this number which represents the amount of time it would take to break even for your business.

So how much marketing capital will you need?

What should be your marketing budget?

That depends on how quickly you want to reach your objective and how well you can keep the customer.

If the customer life is 2 years then you've got to really look at your business model and see if there is anything you can do to:

- Effectively reduce the CoAC.
- Reduce the time from marketing sent to first transaction.

There are ways we could reduce the CoAC, like:

- Beat down the cost of our marketing channels.
- Increase the effectiveness of our marketing message.
- Optimize our list selection.

The first, reducing investment in marketing channels, is NOT one I'd recommend.

While we all want to pay the best price for anything, channels are normally highly competitive and rarely hold large opportunities for profit optimization.

The second and third, the message and the list, are worthy of continual fine tuning, but like most things hold true to the law of diminishing returns. At some point, small tweaks yield result changes so minute they may not be worth your attention at all.

I would suggest that reducing the CoAC, once an effective marketing plan[4] is in place, is NOT where latent profits will be found.

So how do we increase profits through growth without increasing our marketing budget?

And if we can do that, what will happen if we also increase our marketing budget?

Let's say that in order to maintain a consistent customer base of 1,000 customers we have to add 30 new customers each month. At a cost of $200 times 30 new customers per month times 2 months to recoup marketing capital invested we should have $12,000, roughly of marketing capital invested at any point in time.

So, how would you use your $12K to create growth?

What if we could increase the LVoC AND front load that increase, so we don't have to spread it out over 24 months?

Let's suppose that 10 of the 30 new customers would be interested in spending an additional $300 during the first month.

---

4 I don't want to take away from the potential for HUGE gains by addressing message and market. It's well documented that there is enormous potential here. However, the skills necessary to pull significant gains take years to acquire. I'm focusing on the shortest path to higher returns on your time and effort invested, but don't neglect potential in the message and market, just don't expect to master it overnight.

Let's look at what it does with our $12K budget.

With an average of $100 more up front, we can effectively 'reduce' our CoAC to $100!

That means we could invest our same budget and boost our new customers to 60 per month. That's twice as many new customers with the same budget.

Over the course of 2 years, assuming the same atrophy rate, the business would increase the revenue of this company by 72%, while the marketing budget remained the same.

There's a good chance that the owner of our hypothetical business would probably give themselves a raise for being so freaking smart, but would probably add a bit more each month to the marketing budget allowing him or her to triple their revenue even quicker...and maybe, just maybe get to the goal of 4,167 customers!

What if he took 50% of the new revenue generated from his grow during the first 6 months and beefed up his marketing budget?

In one year you would increase your revenue by 170%. Your marketing budget would be up to $34,610.23. And you would've added 1700 new customers. Obviously that kind of growth brings its own problems but still...

Sounds good, right?

But that's only PART of the picture.

Now that I've got you warmed up to my thought process, let me propose that as we increased the revenue for our hypothetical business we didn't increase the profitability in a straight line.

In other words, over the 24 months we would not increase profits by 72% profits as as we increase revenue by 72%. We would increase profitability substantially more. The reason being is there are certain fixed costs of operating any business that rarely are optimized.

Let's look a common institution, the restaurant.

They may be open from 6am to 10pm, but their lease is 24 hours a day. Their equipment costs don't stop at 10pm. Likewise, if they increase their revenue with an up sell, like a large combo, those costs still don't go up.

Fire insurance won't go up because they generated more revenue.

They probably don't have to hire an extra server, cook or manager as a result.

Those costs were there all along, but they were not being tapped out.

Adding the additional revenue only raised one cost, and it wasn't proportional to the revenue increase...food.

OK, the food industry will benefit from up sells.

But what about an intellectual property based business, like information, software, or entertainment?

Generally, aside from marketing costs, the largest cost for these types of businesses is the cost of creating, acquiring the intellectual property. Often this cost doesn't increase as revenue increases, with the exception of licensing, but I'm sure we could outpace that cost exponentially or we have some bad math to deal with.

We could go on and on, but we'll find more of the same trend with varying degrees of profit margin increases with each dollar increase in revenue as we move from industry to industry.

The real key to note here is that with a negative cost of acquisition on a customer, and a fixed marketing budget, by adding an up sell strategy we were able to show that we could substantially grow the revenue of that business over a 2 year time period.

I hope that this scenario is enough for you to recognize the power of adding a single up sell to your business.

It may be enough to excite you. If not, continue reading because believe it or not we haven't even touched on the real power of up sells.

Unfortunately, the real power of up sells may even surpass what most people can conceive that up sells are all about.

This is just the beginning.

Question Time!!!

What is your average CoAC?

_____

_____

What is your average LVoC?

_____

_____

How much capital do you have dedicated to marketing?

_____

_____

How much annual revenue do you really want to produce?

_____

_____

How can you get to that goal using what we discussed in this chapter?

_____

_____

_____

_____

_____

Chapter 7

WHO ARE YOUR MVC's?

Not all customers are created equal. If you communicate with all your customers the exact same way, again call me, I'd love to help you extract all the latent profits that are sitting in your company because you either have no clue who your customers are, or just as bad, you communicate with them all equally.

This question that most often is answered AFTER the customer has been with you for some time.

Oh, I'm sorry, a MVC is a Most Valuable Customer.

They are your super stars and often represent the BEST of your business.

Lose one of these and **you feel it**.

Collect and cultivate a whole herd of them and you FEEL it.

The challenge is often we can't tell who our MVC's are soon enough. We end up communicating and interacting with all our customers equally until we identify the MVC's, then, if we're being intelligent about it, we begin to give MVC's the special attention they require.

But by the time we've noticed who the MVC's are, those who stuck it out, we've probably lost half of the potentially most valuable customers that were available to us.

When you can identify them quickly (*i.e. the first buying interaction*), we change that flat line revenue graph into a front loaded bump with a much higher rate of spending and dramatically increased LVoC.

How do you identify an MVC?

I know we've already spent a bit of time on how up sells can dramatically increase your revenue, not out of sheer volume of revenue derived from up sells alone, but also from increasing your ability to generate more customers from the same marketing budget.

During our discussions that identified some of the indirect benefits of up sells, you may have caught on to the hints as to the method by which we can utilize up sells to identify your most valuable customers early on.

Your MVCs are statistically more likely to be part of the 20-25% that take advantage of your up sell offers. Reason being, they simply are buyers at higher levels. When they have a problem or a dream, they don't hesitate to do whatever it takes to remove the problem or make their dream a reality.

If you personally are a MVC type of person, then you don't need any further explanation. You understand the drive to move forward.

If you are not a MVC type of person, it's extremely important to your success that you first accept the fact that MVC's exist and second do your best to understand what drives them so that you can better serve them.

In the next two chapters we'll go in more depth on the two principle types of MVC's, but for now, at the very least, suspend any doubt and believe that they exist.

For some this may seem like silly talk, but the fact of the matter is that what you BELIEVE about your customers will control how you structure your business.

What do you **BELIEVE** about your customers?

Let me share a quick example that isn't about up sells directly, but that reflect how beliefs about your customers can effect the way you structure your business to your advantage or disadvantage.

My brother and I own a business called Fix Your Funnel that among other things offers a way to communicate with customers through mobile and offline media and integrates with a CRM that we use to automate the marketing of our business.

We were approached and ended up building an integration to this same CRM for a company. We agreed to build out the integration for a flat fee per person who used the integration.

The other company would set up their customers with an account on Fix Your Funnel and then would pay us for each of their customers each month that they used our integration.

As we were discussing the payment process they said that they collected after the service was delivered and that there were a few customers who had not paid for months!

I asked why they didn't have their customers pay in advance. They said that their customers expect to pay after the service is delivered.

They believed that their customers would only pay after the service was delivered. This belief caused them to structure their accounts receivable in a way that reduced their cash on hand. In their particular case I don't think it caused them to be in a precarious financial position, but it could have.

It did change the dynamic of how they interacted with customers. It caused them to feel some resentment toward their customers who may have been behind on paying. This makes it difficult for them to retain those customers.

What would have changed for this business if they had believed that customers would happily pay in advance for their service?

They would have fewer collection issues, since their customers could not fall behind. They would be able to preemptively help customers who were thinking about quitting evaluate if that really was the best decision for them.

Finally, they would be in a better cash on hand position because they were always ahead of the equation. Believe me, being paid in advance is a much nicer position to be in verses trying to stall the people you have to pay for the services you render or products you sell until you can recoup the money you will generate through sales.

I'm not saying that this is the only way to collect revenue, rather the point of this example is that your beliefs about your customers can hinder your ability to be as successful in your business as you'd like.

It's really that simple.

Your MVC's will fall into one of two camps...marathoners and sprinters. Believe it or not I HATE running. In fact I really don't understand what drives a person to just run for exercise.

Personally I LOVE to play basketball. I'll play for hours at a time, running from one end of the court to the other with few breaks.

BUT, I couldn't think of a simple analogy from basketball so I went with running.

Let's take a more in depth look at the two principle types of MVC's, and let's figure out which type you are!

Chapter 8

THE MARATHONER

A marathoner is a special breed of person. They will put their body through a crazy amount of punishment to separate themselves from everyone else on the planet.

Sure, some marathoners may run over 26 miles in a few hours just for the pure enjoyment of it, but I'd venture to guess that a majority do it for one simple reason...to be different.

I think it's just part of our make up as people, we will do the darnedest things to separate ourselves and claim some unique identity.

We want to be reassured that we are unique and we have a purpose.

The marathoner differentiates themselves from the rest of us by being able to travel long distances running. They take extreme pride in being able to do what most can't or won't.

In the MVC context, the marathoner is a VERY special type of customer.

You want to identify them quickly so that you can treat them with the honor and respect they deserve and *expect*.

They're not only high value customers, depending on their referrability index, they can be a tremendous referral source as well.

Marathoners take extreme pride in spending at higher than average levels in any area that interests them. It is a part of their identity.

They not only tend to spend at a higher level than your average customer, but rather than front loading the entire amount, they do it for a VERY LONG period of time. The lifetime customer value of a marathoner is substantially higher than your other customers, including the Sprinter.

Where the Sprinter is hyper, the Marathoner is LOYAL. Once you gain their trust as reflected in the amount of money they spend, unless you loose that trust, they will spend, spend, spend with you.

The Marathoner takes GREAT PRIDE in their loyalty and respond EXTREMELY well to recognition as a long time, premium customer.

Your focus on them must always recognize the extreme value they get, and you enjoy from having them as a customer.

Most companies are lucky to have a few Marathoners. Unfortunately Marathoners are often 'pushed' away by failure to: 1. recognize them and show the respect and appreciation they expect, or 2. failure to provide them with a clear path to buy in the manner they desire.

Failure to recognize the Marathoner early on could result in causing them to feel like their trust has been violated and they'll take their dollars elsewhere.

If you only offer one way for ALL customers to get started with you and keep everyone at the same level of service and interaction, then you will only identify and keep the most patient Marathoners.

How do I identify a Marathoner with an up sell?

This is a common question I get when I teach clients about the Marathoner. You'll get better at it as you gain more experience with up sells, but to begin, find a way to create a VIP experience.

Internally you may think about it as a way to make it easier for them. But never use the word "*EASY*" when engaging the Marathoner. Telling them you'll make it easy takes away from the IMPORTANT part of VIP.

They don't mind being pampered or assisted, but don't make them feel smaller or weaker because they take you up on the offer designed for them. The Marathoner needs to feel a sense of power because they invested in the premium option.

Marathoner's identify with the VIP title, so if there is any way to up your product or service to a VIP experience, offer this as one of your up sells.

Personally, I prefer to present the VIP offer before I present an offer designed to identify and satisfy the Sprinter.

Marathoner's love preferential treatment and have no problem paying for it. Make sure they get the treatment they are after and you'll keep them happy and, if their referrability index is high enough, blabbing about you to everyone they know. This is a good thing because MVCs tend to associate with one another. So a happy Marathoner coupled with an effective strategy for generating referrals can build a business to be envied and sought after.

Chapter 9

THE SPRINTER

Sprinters are fun. Let me start with that. You may be a sprinter. Many business owners are.

The Sprinters tend to be hyper buyers.

When they know what they want, they happily invest to get it. They will take you up on almost any opportunity to get MORE of what they are after...at first.

Because they consume at such high levels they can quickly be satisfied and then move on to the next thing.

Sprinters are good for your business. They can compress the LVoC into a very short period of time. And what's more, they often leave satisfied, so while they won't be with you for a LONG period of time, they will refer happily and speak fondly of their time with you.

If you're not utilizing up sells to effectively satisfy the Sprinter, I guarantee you are loosing out on a LARGE amount of revenue and referral business.

To give you an idea of what a Sprinter's profile might be most closely associated with, think about anyone who is [5]OCD.

The need to have things just so lends to an insatiable appetite to consume services, products, information that will put things in their *"proper order."* I say this with respect (mostly because I identify best with the Sprinter myself).

Since Sprinters are hyper, they tend to be social, so their [6]referrability index generally is MUCH higher. This is a double edged sword.

Bore them and they'll talk about it.

Allow them to ascend quickly and get what they are after, and they will blab about it.

How do I identify a Sprinter with an up sell?

The Sprinter is keenly aware of what the exact problem they are trying to remove or dream they are in pursuit of is. Because of this they are on a MISSION.

---

5 Obsessive-Compulsive Discipline

6 Referrability index is a topic I cover in my book "**4 Cornerstones to a ROCK SOLID Marketing Plan**." If you EVER bring in new customers from WORD of MOUTH, then you MUST understand referrability index, it's to referrals what up sells are to revenue.

You can help them make their mission successful by giving them a path that allows them to get there fast! Where as with the Marathoner your up sell offer is about EASY draped in luxury trappings, for the Sprinter it's all about SPEED.

You can give a single offer that presents the entire 'enchilada', or break up the enchilada into 2 or more parts, so that the varying level of Sprinters can still participate up to the level of their interest.

If you do break up the get there fast up sell into parts, have it be an upgrade with each offer and have a, "*No Thank You*" signal the end of up sells presented, so as to not create a "*No*" set.

It's tempting to want to extract every dime out of the initial transactions, but as a wise man once said, "*Pigs get fat. Hogs go to slaughter.*"

Don't go to slaughter.

You can maximize initial customer value but there is a point at which every dollar you take in an up sell can result in the loss of 2 or 3 dollars in life time value.

Be wise enough to give your various types of customers an opportunity to get what they want, but don't be so aggressive that you ruin the relationship.

There is greater value in increasing initial customer value while identifying your MVCs while not harming the relationship by pushing too hard than there is in maximizing initial customer value.

An example of pushing too hard is offering a down sell at every, "*No*." While no may not mean no when you are in the process of selling to a prospect, once they become a customer and are in the "*Yes*" train of thought, if they say, "*No*" be aware that may mean they are done saying, "*Yes*."

I know that last paragraph can cause issues with those who are aggressive sales people. If that's the case for you, take a breath, and read the last 5 paragraphs again. You'll find I'm not saying don't sell aggressively. I'm saying, you need to be aware of how hard you're pushing and be sensitive enough to the long term relationship that you don't push too far.

Quite honestly, most don't have this problem. Most business owners are way too timid and don't think enough about how to identify MVCs while also increasing initial customer value.

Being able to do both is the sign of the sophisticated business person. It allows you to make other mistakes and still come out smelling like a rose because it stacks the deck in your favor.

Chapter 10

SEGREGATING MVC's

My wife is an avid runner. A couple weeks ago we went to a half marathon that she participated in. There were thousands of runners warming up and the excitement was tangible.

The race was a half marathon with a 5K thrown in for good measure.

The beginner runners think that the 5K is for them, but it's really for the Sprinters.

If I took the top 20-25% of the runners in terms of finish time for the 5K, I'd have the sprinters.

The rest of the 5K runners are the beginners.

The top 20-25% of the runners in terms of finish time from the half marathon are the marathoners.

The rest are the beginners.

If I owned a running store, I'd focus a bulk of my attention on the top two tiers, the sprinters and the marathoners and I'd present different messages to each of them.

They have different interests, desires, needs and emotions they are working to satisfy. If I treated every one that participated in the race the same, I'd be a fool.

Now, please don't take offense by my last statement.

You might have read into that that if you're not segregating your customers into 3 groups, your MVC Sprinters, MVC Marathoners and everyone else and are not communicating to them differently, not presenting offers to them differently, that you're a fool. If you knew that you should be doing that and you have not, then I'm calling you a fool.

If you had never considered the concept and as a result had not implemented it, then I would not consider you a fool. I would consider you a huge success waiting to happen.

Because now that you understand this concept, your competition better watch out! You're about to GO BIG!

Filtering Sprinters from Marathoners

Let's say we're new to the runner business. This is our first race we're putting on.

It's fair to say we probably don't know what message Sprinters will respond to verses the message that Marathoners will respond to.

This could make it difficult to segregate the them before the race begins.

At the Southern California Half Marathon & 5K, you indicated which you type of race you were going to be running when you registered.

But what if they were unable to ask that question?

How could they discover which runner might be a MVC Sprinter or MVC Marathoner?

Could they offer an up sell that was specifically tailored to identify one verses the other?

Marathoners commonly 'eat' nutrient rich goo along the way to prevent their muscles from running out of energy before the end of the course and to prevent cramping.

Sprinters have little use for it.

Beginners may not be aware of the need.

We could offer race registrants the up sell of 3 'goo stops' along the course, where runners could conveniently be handed goo opened and ready for consumption at 3 of over 24 points along the course.

They wouldn't have to fumble with getting the goo out of a pouch, they wouldn't have to try and tear it open, they could simply grab a pouch of goo ready to eat and slurp it down, [7] drop the wrapper on the ground and keep running.

This up sell would definitely segregate our Marathoners from our Sprinters.

But how do we get our MVCs separated from our casual, beginner runners?

Well, one of the major annoyances to the advanced runner (*sprinter or marathoner*) is dealing with large crowds at the beginning of the race.

Some races like to deal with this problem by allowing runners to self determine pace and line up that way, but then you have no certainty that you'll really have people your pace at the beginning of the race.

What advanced runners (*think MVC's*) really want is to be able to begin the race without having to deal with all the amateurs.

Please notice that I'm not thinking about what I have to offer to determine what to up sell.

I'm exploring the desired outcomes and annoyances of the customer.

Always, always, always, always, always start with the customer's desires.

---

7 We would offer disposal service too to make it super attractive to the MVC marathoner.

Now, we have not gone to the deepest level of motivation for our runners in this example. But let's explore a bit more to see if our up sell is the best one to use.

The better we design our up sell, the more likely it is that we'll identify the MVCs, increase our revenue bump and get the results you are after, so NEVER cut corners on this step.

Why does the advanced runner want to be able to start the race without bumping into amateurs? Do they carry communicable diseases? Is it embarrassing to be seen with them? Does it reduce the likelihood that the advanced runner will get what they want?

It is because they advanced runner wants the best time possible. Bumping into amateurs at the beginning effects their time. They could also find it embarrassing to be seen with an amateur ;)

Why does the advanced runner want a good time?

Is it because they want to do their very best?

Or is it because they want to be better than someone else?

Is it because they want to have a GREAT story to tell at some other time?

Is it because they have at some point in their life equated good time with personal value? *"If I run a great race, I'm a better person."*

Once we get to this level, I can't tell for sure exactly what it is that ultimately drives their behavior, but I think we were able to nail it down to a handful of possibilities.

How helpful are these possibilities in determining the value of our up sell to the prospect?

How well can we hypothesize that the outcome will tell us something about the buyer?

My first up sell to a race registrant would be to offer them an opportunity to begin the race 5 minutes before the rest of the registrants.

Now, it's true, I will get some amateurs that will take my up sell, not because they are advanced, but because they are MVC Sprinters in the true sense of the word, not in the race sense of the word.

But the bulk of the folks that take me up on the head start up sell will be my "*advanced*" MVCs.

The second up sell I'd offer would be the goo stations. That should then separate my marathoners from my sprinters.

By carefully designing my offers to match the needs and desires of my prospective clients, I'm able to quickly identify my prospective Most Valuable Clients and their hot points.

These two up sells, if offered to all registrants would create 4 groups; the standard racers, the advanced sprinter MVC, the advanced marathoner MVC and the beginner marathoner MVC.

I would be wise to mark these customers with clear marks that would tell me how I should communicate in the future with them in the future in order to optimize sales and their experience.

Now would be an excellent opportunity for you to reconsider your primary products and services and who consumes them.

What drives them?

What do they REALLY want? Articulate it one more time:

_____

_____

_____

_____

Remember, they don't really want[8] your product or service, they want what they think your product or service will give them.

Fold over this page, you'll want to reference it later.

---

8 If you still believe that they really do want your product or service for what it is and nothing more, then play a quick game with me. Let's pretend that your customer really does want something more than your product or service. Let's pretend that they wanted something that they imagined your product or service would give them. What is that? What is the feeling, need met, status obtained that comes from investing in your product or service?

Now don't start creating up sell offers yet!

I really don't want you to begin creating a list of potential up sells just right yet. Let your mind bounce around ideas, but let's not give them full life on paper yet. Your up sells are still formulating, growing and curing.

However, you can begin to brainstorm the base needs and desires that your customers believe your product or service will satisfied or meet.

Notice I said "believe."

What your customer believes is more important that what reality may be.

If you sell a line of clothing, your customer may believe that wearing your clothing makes the appear sophisticated and wealthy. Looking wealthy may make them feel important and valuable.

Reality is that feeling important or valuable are not connected to what you wear. You inherently have value and are important by [9] birth. Your worth may be enhanced because of your choices, but certainly not by your appearance.

---

9 Not because of your earthly parents. Rather as a child of God with unlimited potential to become like Him, you have value regardless of who your parents are, what you wear, what education you have pursued. Your choices to respect others, be kind, honest, etc can modify your importance and ultimate potential, which ultimately is the value you place upon yourself.

However, what is real doesn't matter to the customer. Their actions will be motivated by what they desire and believe.

Reality isn't even a consideration.

As business owners we can't spend our time evaluating if the motivations of our customers are right or wrong. Our responsibility begins and ends with the ethics of what we offer.

Does what we offer provide value to the marketplace?

Is it legal?

Is it consistent with our personal values?

Yes? Yes? Yes?

Then let's go forward at full power.

Let's go back to the race example.

From the perspective of a running store, the benefit of the up sells we laid out, is a segregation of the customer list into advanced sprinters, advanced marathoners and beginner runners.

This would allow the running store to approach the runners based on where they are and the known problems they want to resolve.

But what about the race promoters? What if we were to create the up sells from their perspective? What would be the greatest advantage to the promoter beyond the revenue bump?

Let's think it through together.

The base challenges of the runners don't change just because the business perspective is different. So let's suppose that the solutions we provided before are what we're working with. What do these two offers do for the race promoter?

Up sell 1: Goo Stations

Up sell 2: Head Start

Anytime you can make your MVC's lives easier, you win long term relationship foundation. The stronger your foundation the more benefits can come to your business. Now, as a race promoter, we would have asked the runners to indicate if they were interested in running the 5K or the half marathon.

The main thing that the head start up sell would do is allow us to identify who we should be work with first to register for our next race. It would also allow us to be able to approach product suppliers that would be of interest to advanced runners and broker offers we could make to our customers.

Goo stations would allow us to segregate the distance runners who are more pre disposed to spend for ease, and should allow us to plan a VIP experience at a higher price for our next race and pre sell it to these runners.

Now let's consider another way to use up sells unrelated to our runner example. Let's talk about a live event...not a race.

Let's suppose that you are selling tickets to a training, convention, or other gathering that will be filled with customers. Let's suppose further that we never offered up sells to these customers, so as far as we can tell they are equal. What if we wanted to identify our MVCs? How would we do it?

What would we need to do, to find out who has more disposable income and are inclined to invest in higher end experiences?

When we run an event our first up sell is quantity. We register one person, and the first up sell is the opportunity to bring guests. The reason this comes first will be apparent when you consider up sell number two.

Next we offer VIP experience. We offer this second to give the customer the opportunity to upgrade their experience AND the experience of some or all of their guests. This is VERY important.

We NEVER make money on the VIP up sell. We utilize ALL of what we charge to give the VIP's the best possible experience. WHY?

Isn't the point to make money? Aren't we in business to make as much money as we ethically can??

ABSOLUTELY!

But NEVER, EVER, EVER allow short term profits to prevent you from receiving long term equity. When we reinvested every dime we charged for VIP into VIP, our goal was to create stronger relationship with our MVCs.

A stronger relationship with our customers and in particular our MVCs is worth many multiples of the VIP up sell. Additionally if you are good at selling in an event environment, your VIPs have self identified themselves as those who are able to spend. Special preparation for the sale should be directed toward the VIPs.

This is another HUGE principle that CANNOT AND SHOULD NOT be overlooked. Your marketing dollars should never been spent equally on all your prospects. A MVC will bring 4 to 5 times as much of your revenue as your average customer. A repeat customer is more valuable than a brand new customer.

Your marketing dollars should be invested in that [10]order.

1st priority is your MVC.

2nd priority is your repeat customer.

3rd priority is the new customer.

Up sells are most useful to direct your marketing dollars.

---

10 Don't even begin to think that this order is complete or the end all say all. In my book, **4 Cornerstones of a Rock Solid Marketing Plan** I layout the complete order and hierarchy of where your marketing dollars ought to be spent.

Chapter 11

INCREASING INITIAL CUSTOMER VALUE ONLINE

There are two forms of selling online; those that require a shopping cart and those that don't.

Those that don't are purchases that are made through what is known as an online order form (I'll just call it order form for short).

The real difference between an order form and a shopping cart is the number of steps; the order form tends to be a single step for the customer and the shopping cart requires multiple page views or steps before the initial transaction is completed.

My personal preference when selling online is creating a situation where you don't have to use a shopping cart. But that's not always possible.

The reasons I like the order form over the shopping cart are:

I know human nature well enough to realize that prospects are not good at following complicated instructions. The more you require of the customer to part with their money, the more you will loose prospects in the process.

Studies have shown from 60-70% of all potential orders are abandoned in the shopping cart. I'll be first to admit that a good number or portion of these 'abandonments' were probably not buyers at all but rather tire kickers who were trying to find out price.

In fact 74% of shopping cart abandonments happen at the shipping price portion of the cart. So a good number may be the same people who buy, but first check out price with shipping and then come back later and buy for real.

Regardless, even when a person is highly motivated, why would you add any additional steps between them and their giving you their money than are absolutely necessary and are not specifically designed to create some benefit to you as the seller?

And what's more, the prospect that doesn't buy your initial offer, can't possibly become a customer. And if they can't become a customer, they certainly can't upgrade their order with your up sell. And if they can't upgrade their initial order, then you can't possibly identify them as a Most Valuable Customer, so you're really up a creek!

Michele Catalano @inthefade   16 Jun
Went to buy something online, ordering took me to page with more products. Page was titled "**upsell**" - I got insulted and canceled.
Expand ← Reply ⇄ Retweet ★ Favorite

Michele was up sold before she completed the first transaction; but what's worse, inside language was used outside. Just because it is an up sell doesn't mean you call it one.

If you're selling online and have used a shopping cart as a matter of convenience rather than necessity due to your business model...switch now!

The software I use in my businesses to handle our online transactions, subscriptions and other e-commerce needs is also our CRM[11].

I use our CRM to handle all our e-commerce needs because it removes the need for multiple systems to communicate in order to automate confirmation and delivery of orders initiated through an online order form or one click up sells.

Another reason I choose order forms whenever possible is it allows me to control the point of entry and the customer experience all the way through the sales process.

I don't believe in relying upon random initial purchasing by my customers. I will always provide a way for the

---

11 CRM is short for client relationship management software. It use to be somewhat optional for a business, but no longer. In order to stay remotely compedative today you MUST find one that works for you and employ it to it's fullest potential.

random prospect that discovers my website to buy if they like, but I don't allow that to prevent me from creating a very specific set of points of entry.

The Yellow Brick Road

I want to prepare a yellow brick road for my new customers so they don't get lost before they arrive at my Emerald City (*that's what I call my cash register*).

I'm not alone in my philosophy about client acquisition. If you'd like an example, turn on talk radio or open up a tabloid. I guarantee you'll run into an ad that showcases a single product.

The uninitiated may believe that the product showcased is the ONLY product that company sells. Or that they really are giving away free samples simply for a study.

What they are really doing is creating a simple yellow bring road for the prospect to follow to their Emerald City. However, the difference between Dorothy's yellow brick road and the road you want to build, is there are no scary forests, or flying monkeys.

In fact, that is the reason why I prefer to build my yellow brick road verses letting the prospect decide what their initial experience will be like. I want to reduce distractions and concerns to an absolute minimum in order to create a controlled environment where my carefully prepared steps can allow me to groom and prepare the prospect to become an ideal customer as they get exactly what they want as fast as they want to get it.

Do you present the up sells before, with or after the initial order online?

This is the most common question I hear when discussing up sells online.

There are plenty of high profile examples of companies that offer up sells before and after the initial transaction. Amazon.com 'suggests', with social proof, that you add to your order, before you check out. They also will suggest additional products to purchase after you check out.

They don't do this for fun, or hoping. They have tones of data backing up their decision to offer before and after. They also use algorithms to determine what to show to whom at each time.

Due to the nature of their business model, they can't create a yellow brick road and direct their prospect to a single order form, so a shopping cart makes the most sense. I add this example for two reasons.

First, if you have a business model that is similar to Amazon's, where you are a distributer for a vast number of products and or services from a vast number of sources, then building yellow brick roads becomes very complicated. It therefore makes sense to go with the shopping cart option from a sanity standpoint alone.

Second, to illustrate that every rule has exceptions. Rules are generalized statements and life is highly complicated. Rules can appear to be in direct conflict with each other, but when the why is understood than you can make adjustments where it's prudent.

Let me take this further...I have some programming and development experience, so as I was writing the paragraphs above I thought of a way that you could program Amazon's algorithms into a application that would allow you to create a site that would allow for an infinite number of possible yellow brick roads, which could be built on the fly to accommodate a particular search phrase or term.

I won't go further into this, but I will say that what may drive one person insane and cause them to throw their hands up in the air and yell, *"Forget it!"* could be the problem that is solved by another person's innovation and [12]flip an old rule on it's ear forever.

My Rule for When to Up Sell Online

My personal preference is for the post initial order up sell.

The last thing I want to do while seeking to increase initial customer value is scare off the customer in the first place!!

A common practice, online, is to add things to the order before the prospect has even become a customer. Admittedly there may be reasons you would want to do this.

---

12 Flipping rules on their ears is a topic of another book I have coming out later this year, so keep an eye out for it if you pick up this book when it's released or look it up if you buy this book after the fall of 2012.

If you're trying to tip your hand to the MVC's that there is more they can do with you beyond your initial offer, this may cause you to want to present an up sell before the initial order.

I really have no problem with this, so long as you don't devaluate the standard offer in the process. A real temptation in these situations is to make the standard initial offer look too basic so that the prospect is ashamed to buy it. If the MVC offer is not a match for the prospect then you may scare them off from becoming a customer at all.

I want to remind you that while a majority of your MVC's will be identified through your up sells, not all will. Some are incubated. Some are formed through the results they get out of what you offer. So the last thing we want to do is sacrifice life time value while trying to increase initial customer value.

A prospect who never becomes a customer, buy who would have if not for our pre initial order up sell, has a life time value of zero. Mission Fail.

Everyone loves to reinforce a good decision.

If you bought a new car today, you would want to feel reassured that you made the right decision.

It's human nature.

When you don't feel reassured, you experience a sensation called *"buyer's remorse."*

You don't like this feeling as a customer, you should hate it as a seller.

Look, I know you want a long term success, not a flash in the pan. I don't think any right thinking person of integrity and honor wants a fly by night, one sale and on to the next victim type of business.

I know that because you're reading this book.

So since that's the case, then you want your customer to feel confident in what they purchased. The strongest method to feel assured in a buying decision, interestingly enough, is to make another buying decision.

It's because of this reinforcement of your first good decision to buy by the second good decision to buy, that I prefer to have all my up sells post initial transaction.

In fact, while it's true I use up sells to segregate my MVC's from the rest of the customers, whenever it's possible, I try and create a simple no-brainer up sell that most of my customers can take me up on simply to activate this physiological decision reinforcer.

All of this hangs on adherence to the ideas we've laid out so far in this book. Your up sell offers HAVE to be congruent with the identified problem your customer wants to avoid or the dream they are pursuing.

How Much Copy To Connect The Dots?

It depends on how well you've sold the story of your solution approach to the customer. If the customer gets you and you've connected with them on the initial sale, then you really need as little copy as it takes to connect the dots.

Remember that at the point of the post initial transaction up sell, you want to maintain the, "*Yes*" momentum through the process and keep them headed down the Yellow Brick Road.

> *If you're selling online or are getting ready to start selling online and would like to discuss how to put the rubber to the road with up sells, regardless of which software or system you want to use or are using, call (760) 452-8555 and we'll arrange a time to review your situation and make sure you have the bases covered.*

Why I wrote a script for one click up sells for InfusionSoft in 2009.

Now that you know my preferences for offering up sells online, you also know why I was driven to write a script that has generated millions in revenue for small businesses across the world.

> *I want to share with you what I wrote into my script and the why behind it so that as you set your solution into place you can benefit from the lessons I learned.*

Returning to the yellow brick road analogy, when I'm leading the prospect to the initial order, my road extends beyond the first order. I want my yellow brick road to enter the glistening green gates of Emerald City and lead the all the way to the Wonderful Wizard's court.

That means I not only reduce any interaction that isn't absolutely necessary between the prospect and the initial order, I also remove additional work for the new customer as they are presented with opportunities to take me up on my up sells.

With a new prospect I HAVE to ask for their credit card number and contact information in order to be able to process the initial order and deliver the goods or services, but once I have that information, I don't want them to have to pull the credit card back out or fill out another form unless it's completely necessary.

So when I was searching for a technological solution to meet my requirements I had already decided I was using InfusionSoft to handle my e-commerce needs.

All that I needed was a simple way to offer a single click up sell.

I waited for a full year before I broke down and wrote the script that makes this possible.

I made it so simple to use that anyone could use it.

Then when other business owners heard I'd built it, they begged me to sell them a copy for their own online sales.

Obviously, I obliged.

Security Concerns

While I was waiting for someone to write the script I ended up writing, I heard about a number of *'shady'* methods being used to make one click up sells work.

All of them involved passing customer credit card numbers in ways that were not secure. There's nothing about that idea that makes sense. In fact it's a sure fire recipe for disaster. If you're going to offer up sells online, make sure that you're not tossing around people's financial information.

I utilize InfusionSoft's API to create and charge orders inside of InfusionSoft. Sensitive information is never exposed to prying eyes and in spite of the lack of sensitive information, secure connections with the corresponding encryption are always used.

Individual Transactions

My script creates an individual transaction for each up sell order. This has good and bad points. The good is that each order could be verified as successful immediately so the customer could continue down the yellow brick sales road with confidence that they would receive what they had purchased.

As a seller, I could be confident that when I initiated the delivery of the promised product and or service using the automation in InfusionSoft, that the money had been collected in advance or as anticipated.

The bad side could come from multiple transaction fees with your merchant account provider as each up sell was it's own transaction. If you have tight profit margins or low price points, it could be significant factor.

Unique Merchant Account for each Up Sell

The script also allowed the merchant account to use for the specific up sell to be adjusted on an offer by offer basis. For companies with multiple merchant accounts dedicated to different business activities, this was a real bonus.

Most businesses are satisfied with a single merchant account, but the dangers of this are only well known to businesses that experience tremendous growth. It's not uncommon for a merchant to hold on to ten or hundreds of thousands of dollars of revenue for months when explosive growth occurs.

It's a matter of risk management on the merchant account provider's part, but can really cramp your style if you're not prepared for it.

Automated Delivery

Obviously how what is offered will be delivered varies from business to business, but regardless of what you offer, the delivery can and ought to be automated as much as possible. Even if all you can automate is the assigning of a task to the person who will perform the service to initiate setting an appointment.

I connected a successful transaction to the initiating of an InfusionSoft follow up sequence, which can contain a series of steps that are timed to deliver email, fax, voice broadcast, text message, mailing a greeting card, postcard or gift, assigning a task to a staff member, creating an account on a website, etc.

Their list of automated actions continues to grow and be expanded by [13]third parties.

The reason this is so important when selling online and particularly when up selling online is because the quicker you confirm an order and begin delivery the more assured the customer feels.

Utilizing multiple medias in your confirmation and delivery insures that you communicate with the new customer (MVC in the case of our up sells) in a way that will deliver the message effectively.

One Click Up Sell

In the very beginning of the life of the script it was truly a single click on the new customer's part to say, "*Yes*" to the up sell. But that turned out to be more like a yellow brick slide than a yellow brick road. Maybe even a yellow brick trap door!

---

13 One of my companies, FixYourFunnel, extends the automated actions to include SMS, and mailing greeting cards, postcards and gifts.

I had to refund too many *'accidental'* buyers that I realized that curiosity may have driven some new customers to click on the buy link just to see what would happen.

As a result I added a pop up confirmation that allowed them to click again before they would be charged. Now as I'm writing this I realize I probably should change the name of it to *"One Click Followed By A Confirmation Click Up Sell Script"*, but that just seems too long.

The confirmation restated what they were about to buy and the price that would be charged to their card. That was the trick to virtually eliminate 'accidental' purchases.

"No Thanks" Links

You'll recall that one of the common mistakes is offering too many up sells. The use of a *"No Thanks"* link on your up sell pages allows non-MVC's to self identify so that you don't have to drag a non-MVC through too many up sells.

I track my no thank you clicks so that I can test my up sells. If you don't track who abandons or doesn't take you up on your up sell offers, then it makes it impossible to adjust your offers.

Even if you get every concept laid out in this book and are confident that you've nailed it with your offers, testing is the last word when it comes to up sells.

I do everything I can when creating a yellow brick sales road, but once I begin to send real prospects and new customers down that road I'm paying careful attention to verify that my theory about how my new customers would respond is accurate.

If I see response that is outside of the 20-25% uptake range, I should expect, for an up sell designed to identify a MVC, then I have to reevaluate the offer. I have to look at the price, what's included, how I'm presenting it and determine if I'm making a common mistake.

You can make a change to early, so you do need to have a little patience before making a final decision. Make sure that you allow a statistically significant number of your buyers down the road before you make any decisions.

Review all of your goals for your up sells and how your results match up before testing a change. Failing to give your up sells a chance is as big a mistake as ignoring them completely.

The only exception to the rule of giving your up sells time is if you realize that you committed one of the common mistakes, then by all means fix it. But once you've made the correction...let it ride for a while.

Wordpress Integration

I recently upgraded the script to include Wordpress integration. I did this to make it really easy for the non-coder business owner to complete the implementation process without the annoying delays that inevitably occur when you bring in techies.

With whatever solution you find for allowing you to create up sells online, make sure that it's Wordpress easy for you to create and modify your up sell offers.

The smart business owner wants to keep the up sell adjusting available and understandable by them.

More Information

If you're using InfusionSoft already and your business model will work with order forms, then you may want some information on the script I wrote.

Text the word **SCRIPT** *to* **(760) 452-8555**...

...and I'll send you a link to the latest information about the script.

Last Word About Online Up Sells

The biggest mistake you can make online is to invest a lot of time and money before you prove your concept. Spend as little time and money as possible to test your concept before you worry about really beefing it up.

I've seen a goodly number of folks think they have a great idea. They finally get the courage up to pursue their dream and then fall for the oldest trick in the book. Invest too much time, money and effort into an unproven model only to pitifully discover they were not even in the right time zone, much less the right ballpark.

Prove your concept, then ramp it up. You'll get to the point of proving your concept faster and you'll most likely have the money from sales to pay for ramping up your idea.

Chapter 12

THE ULTIMATE UP SELL OPPORTUNITY

Up selling offline is the most powerful environment you can imagine. Interestingly enough, what makes it so powerful can also make it wildly inconsistent.

For all the benefits of offering up sells online, like the controlled reveal of the next up sell, it is purely logical in it's function.

Currently the technology to really intelligently capture rich feedback and adjust the up sell presented online doesn't exist for the average business.

Contrast that to the experience I had at lunch today.

I normally drive home and enjoy lunch with my wife and any of my children who are home at the time. It's one of the luxuries I enjoy.

Today I was not so fortunate. The car is in the shop, my wife was running errands and so I kept working through lunch until my stomach reached up and slapped me in the face.

So at 2pm I borrowed one of my staff's cars and drove through a fast food joint. The woman on the other end of the microphone, who I know is paid less than $12/hour began to take my order.

"I'll have the number 4."

What she said back caused a grin the size of Texas to cross my face.

"Would you like to go large?"

He he he. What could I say. I was starving (my problem) and I wanted to be full (my dream), plus she just said the name of my book! What could I say???

"Yes. Yes, I do."

I did drink the entire soda. However, I can see the cold fries on the conference room table from my desk. Guess I better throw that away on my way out.

They picked up an extra 89 cents. Probably cost them 9 at most. That's 13 cents a word. May not seem like much, but that happens many times each day and it adds up on the bottom line.

You can guarantee she learned that script the first day she was trained for the coveted order taking position.

Now I mean no disrespect to the kind woman at the fast food joint. I was very glad she took the job today, because I got the food I wanted.

But if she can be taught to say those 6 magic words, words in a language she wasn't born speaking (*if you have learned a foreign language your respect for her should have gone up even further...I learned Portuguese living in Rio De Janeiro Brazil for two years, so I appreciate what that means*), is there anyone in your company that can't learn an up sell script?

That all being said, if our fast food order taking lady wasn't monitored and retrained consistently, eventually the benefit of those 6 words may be lost on her and I guarantee she'd quit asking.

Unfortunately, this fast food joint is really close to my office. I've been there all too often when lunch at home didn't work out.

Today's six words isn't the best script I've heard. You know the best one I've heard:

"Would you like to make that a medium or a large?"

The inexperienced may be tempted to say, *"Isn't giving an option worse than offering only the large?"* or *"What if you offered the medium if they say no to the large?"*

If you were tempted to say that, then you probably should consider what we discussed in chapter 3 about too many up sells.

In some offline sales environments we only have a few seconds to offer our up sell, such as the drive thru. If that's the case then we can't afford to create a mini "*No*" set.

We'll get more mediums and large up sells sold by offering one of two up sells than we will just offering the largest. And what's more, the profit percentage is about the same with the medium and large.

By giving these two options and presenting them as though the customer needs to select one or the other is a great way to help customers who are interested in accelerating their progress to make a decision when they are sitting on the fence.

Because the double bind is so powerful you need to make an ethical decision before you employ it. Would it be in your customer's best interest to accelerate their journey to realizing their dream or relieving their problem? If you customer will be better off then you have an obligation to help your customers fight against human nature and make a decision.

Customer's natural inclination is to delay the purchase decision, which generally means they fail to progress toward what they really want. This is not a good outcome for anyone. It extends misery from an unresolved problem or delays the realization of a dream and the joy and fulfillment that comes with it.

Once the customer is in a decision making mood, the double bind can help them to continue in the productive direction by reducing the decision to which good option they should choose.

If you're selling offline, what up sells could you offer in a double bind?

_____

_____

_____

_____

_____

Write out your own double bind script:

_____

_____

_____

_____

_____

Final Thoughts on Offline Up Sells

One thing I want to point out about offline is the process for creating the up sell paths is the exact same as for online. The only difference is that you have more options for determining which up sells should be presented to which customers, which leads to a much more effective design of the up sell path.

Generally online you don't have the feedback beyond the yes and no to determine which up sells to offer and the resulting experience for the customer. The limitations online in determining what to offer can make a big difference in bottom line results.

Finally, when it comes to up selling offline, there are so many examples around you that you can use that I highly recommend that you keep a journal on up sells you are presented.

Note how well they apply the concepts in this book.

Note the language they use to present the offers.

As you dedicate yourself to become a serious student of up sells in all their environments you'll be able to leverage all the opportunities available to you through up sells.

Chapter 13

OFFERING UP SELLS TO GROUPS

Selling in groups is really an extension of selling offline we covered in the last chapter with a few distinctions worth of it's own discussion.

Up sells in groups includes selling via direct mail as well as selling to groups in a live presentation. Generally this is done with a paper form doing most of the heavy lifting.

With each environment, online, offline, one on one and up selling to groups, there are trade offs and advantages.

One of the biggest disadvantages to the paper order form verses the online order form is it's inability to segment offer presentation.

In contrast to online where we can segment and only show one up sell at a time and change that path online, we don't have that same luxury with the paper form.

The interesting fact is that even though you have those limitations with the paper form, about 21% of people presented with an up sell on a paper form will still take you up on the offer.

So it's still really about identifying the most valuable customers and then providing them with ways to accelerate their progress.

Up sells in a paper format can be as simple as a checkbox next to a description of the offer.

In interviews I've had with highly successful direct response marketers they've told me that they have been able to offer up sells from $2,000 to $20,000 on paper order forms distributed in groups or via direct mail just by adding a simple checkbox at the bottom of a paper order form.

And what really makes this interesting is that independently of each other they all reported 20-25% as the typical result.

Phraseology

As important as the words you use in the sales process face to face and with your online order forms are, it's even more important with the paper order form.

You don't have the ability to read the face of the customer and make adjustments.

You have to pay particular attention to how the wording in your copy on the enrollment form reduces feelings of fear and risk. You need to make sure that what you write puts people at ease and reverses risk.

Is the copy on your form focused on what you get out of the relationship or on what protects you? If so, do a 180 and figure out how to make it all about the customer and putting them at ease.

You can probably take what used to protect you and make it so that it sounds like a benefit to them.

Add guarantees that have teeth.

If you're confident in what you offer, find a way to express that with a guarantee that penalizes you severely if you fail to deliver, but that you are more confident that you can prevent from ever happening.

Make the guarantee *outrageous.*

For one company we had a "*Jump in a pit of alligators naked Guarantee.*"

It stated that if after 90 days the new customer wouldn't happily jump into a pit of alligators naked to wrestle away our product, because it was that valuable to them, then we would gladly refund them every cent...no questions asked.

I didn't make up the guarantee.

I heard it and borrowed it.

But only because I was happy to honor it. Did we have refunds? Yes. Was it because we couldn't deliver. No. I really think some folks have a tremendous fear of alligators.

Some people call it risk reversal, but regardless of what you call it, find a way to incorporate it into your up sells on paper and life will be much better for you.

Of course, you ought to be using that in all your up sells and initial sell situations.

Even the fonts you use can have a big impact.

We had a hired gun, that's code for front of the room salesman, who had an awesome record, to consult with a speaker/salesman we had traveling for one of our companies.

As part of the consultation he reviewed everything that came into play with the bottom line result.

One of the things he told us to change was the font on our forms. *"This font you're using looks like work and it's intimidating. Your buyers need to feel like they can do what it is they want to do more easily with your help. Your copy communicates that, but the font conflicts with the message."*

At first I balked, but then I looked at the form with fresh eyes and realized he was right. We immediately changed the form and saw a bump in sales as a result.

From that day forward, I've always made sure that the typography of my enrollment forms is congruent with the message and feeling I want them to communicate.

Is your up sell exclusive?

Using exclusivity will attract your marathoners. Remember that marathoners want the feeling of luxury and one of the key characteristics of luxury is exclusivity.

Find ways to weave exclusivity into your forms and presentations.

Exclusivity can be reached by price point as well as a limited number of customers that will be able to acquire the offer.

Exclusivity only works when it makes complete and total sense to the prospective buyer that the limitation is not artificially controlled.

If your reason for creating exclusivity isn't legitimate, it holds no power to attract the buyers you want. Beyond that it damages your integrity.

To create authentic exclusivity use mediums that are clearly in limited supply and attach them to your offer.

Time

There's only 24 hours in a day. Ain't no one except theoretically physicists that will argue that one. So ask yourself how can your offer be attached to the limited resource of time in order to create exclusivity.

I have a friend that structures one of his highest price up sells around 1 on 1 time with him. He obviously only have so much time available, and between positioning and disposition he will only allow so much of that to be available for fulfilling the offer, so he can create legitimate exclusivity and limitation on the number of the up sell he can make available at any given point in time.

Space

When introducing a done for you marketing program we couldn't put ourselves in a position to work for two people in the same geographic region and in the same niche at the same time. We would literally be competing against ourselves on behalf of our customers.

Space or rather geography is fixed, unless Al Gore is correct, in which case it's decreasing. Either way, it ain't growing, so it's limited in supply and offers a legitimate foundation for exclusivity.

Even if space travel and colonization took off, space continues to be a limiting factor as with today's technology no two things can occupy the same space at the same time.

We might have more locations we could sell to, but the competition for each space remains intense, making it a perfect candidate for creating exclusivity.

Resources

My wife recently turned me onto this show called **Hollywood Treasures** which is like a high end version of **American Pickers**. Two shows I enjoy because of the salesmanship that goes on in each episode.

Each show highlights the value generated by exclusivity because of a genuine limited resource. In this case, collectable items that are one of a few or one of kind and can't be replicated and hold the same value.

The value is intrinsic to it's rarity.

What element of your offer can be connected to a limited resource beyond time and space?

Write down legitimate limitations you can place on your highest value up sell to create genuine exclusivity:

_____

_____

_____

_____

_____

_____

Chapter 14

NO SIMPLE ANSWERS

I hope you've enjoyed the book. More importantly I hope you've already begun to put the concepts to work for you.

Before I close out this book I wanted to touch on one last topic that is critical to lasting success. So much so that I dedicated an entire chapter to it. And that is...

Everyone wants a simple answer.

They want something they can fit in a thimble and apply to a thousand scenarios.

I was preparing for the workshop I mentioned in chapter 5 and I had a member of my staff call 100 of our members to see what they thought they wanted to get from a workshop on marketing.

The responses disturbed me at first.

"I just want Ryan to give me marketing pieces, tell me exactly who to mail them to, when to mail them and then exactly what to say when the leads call. That's it."

For years I'd been teaching this group how to write copy, how to select a list, how to determine how many and how often to mail. I'd shared sample marketing pieces and maps of marketing processes to set up and implement. I'd taught them how to handle the sales appointment to set positioning and eliminate concerns.

In spite of all that I had taught them, apparently much to involved and complicated to be easily implemented, what they wanted was a simple answer.

Like I said, initially, I was disturbed at their answer.

Then I realized it was human nature.

We couldn't possibly have selected the only people on the planet who would ask for the exact same thing. Most people must want the simple answer. The step by step recipe that requires no thought, no consideration.

I gave them what they wanted.

But I laced it with the foundational concepts...just in case.

There are such things as principles, concepts which may be applied to a myriad of situations with anticipated outcome, but often when overly simplified they can appear to be in conflict.

I hope that you don't fall prey to relying on simple answers.

The reality is that life is complicated and simple at the same time.

Success is both complicated and simple at the same time.

But neither are just simple nor complicated.

Because they have both, you can't afford to cling to just one truth and expect to make your dreams come true and eliminate the problems that plague you.

The answers are found in simple principles and often complex solutions...but never in simple answers.

Making Sense of Conflicting Concepts

Recognize that anything you thing you know as a fact that seems to be in conflict with what you may have understood from this book most likely isn't in conflict with this book at all.

The physicist's view of the world includes a truth that conflict does not exist.

Any where that you perceive conflict to exist is the result of an untrue assumption.

Take a look at the two thoughts that seem to be in conflict and determine what assumptions are made that create the conflict.

Challenge the assumptions.

Ask if they are reality or fiction created to fill in the gaps where you did not have all the information you needed.

135

When you do, you will discover that the underlying assumptions about one of the conflicting ideas is the source of the conflict. The assumptions were not accurate.

Eliminate or adjust the assumptions to match reality and you will have resolved the conflict.

This may be why I love business and marketing strategy so much. It allows us to create something truly remarkable as we hypothesize, test and discover how to pull together all the pieces of a business to create immense value for other people, and as a result ourselves.

Personally, I'm a praying man. I pray with my wife and children each morning and night. Invariably, business is pulled into our prayers. Often it's me asking God for insight into how I can create more value for more people in more creative ways.

I pray your journey in business is a profitable one for you and your customers.

Remember, make it easier for your customers to get what they REALLY want and you will enjoy greater success at higher levels than ever before.

Increasing initial customer value, without sacrificing life time value, is simply the result of doing that one thing the right way.

-RJC

Do you have a group?

Do you have a group or organization that you'd like to expose to Ryan's message from this book?

Call (760) 452-8555 to arrange his appearance at your event.

Do you have a business ready to hit new levels?

Do you have a business that hasn't realized the full power of up sells and you'd like to have Ryan review what it is you offer to the market place and help you structure up sells that will increase profit, allow you to crush your competition and identify your most valuable customers as they buy for the first time?

Call (760) 452-8555 to arrange an appointment to speak with Ryan.

Are you setting up an online sales process?

Are you setting up an online sales process and want Ryan's years of insight to help you know if your up sells are increasing life time value or killing it?

Call (760) 452-8555 to arrange an appointment to speak with Ryan.

Are you putting on a live event where you plan to sell?

Oh man...up sells are a secret weapon that Ryan has used over and over again to choreograph live sales performances that are optimized to create high closing percentages.

This isn't done by 'tricking' attendees into buying (no mind control or buyer's remorse; only high trust/ relationship building actions), but rather by using advanced versions of the concepts laid out in this book to identify and interact with MVCs in order to maximize profits from efforts put forth.

If you are putting on a live event and you don't know how to use up sells to choreograph your sales opportunities, then you must call (760) 452-8555 to arrange an appointment to speak with Ryan.

Made in the USA
Charleston, SC
08 August 2012